Besties AMAZING SUPER SECRETS

Created by
Mickey & Cheryl Gill

Fine Print Publishing Company
P.O. Box 916401
Longwood, Florida 32791-6401

This book is printed on acid-free paper.
Created in the USA & Printed in China

ISBN 978-1-892951-74-8

2 4 6 8 10 9 7 5 3 1

fprint.net

Besties
AMAZING
SUPER
SECRETS

Quizzes, Questions
& Secret PassNotes

FINE print
PUBLISHING

YOU'VE JUST ENTERED A

TOTES SECRET

AND SOMETIMES INVISIBLE

WORLD.

TAKE QUIZZES, ANSWER SOME QUESTIONS,
AND DISCOVER YOU AND YOUR BESTIES' SUPER SECRETS!

USE YOUR INVISIBLE PEN

Make it
invisible!

WHEN YOU SEE SPY GIRL ON A PAGE.
THEN SHINE THE PEN LIGHT ON
WHAT YOU WRITE.
NOW YOU DON'T SEE IT,
NOW YOU DO.

SEND BESTIES SECRET PASSNOTES

TO ALL YOUR FRIENDS.
FIND THEM IN THE BACK OF THIS BOOK.

Name most people call you?

Nickname?

- ○ Keep things to yourself
- ○ Share stuff with your BFF
- ○ Tell everyone everything?

Who's your BFF?

Best place for hiding your favorite stuff?

Something you're not afraid of that most people are?

Do you
- ○ stick your nose in your friends' business
- ○ respect your friends' space?

Would you rather have a
- ○ phone watch
- ○ night vision goggles
- ○ secret recording ring?

Language you'd love to learn?

Disguise you'd be willing to wear?

- ⊙ sunglasses and mustache
- ⊙ ninja suit
- ⊙ gorilla costume

Choose some accessories to start your mission!

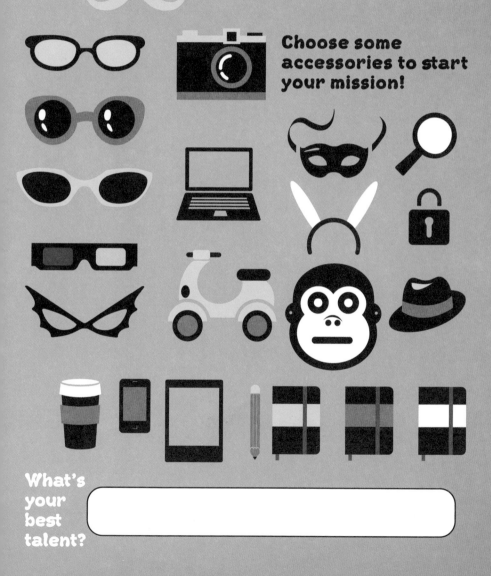

What's your best talent?

ASK SOME

QUESTIONS

& TAKE SOME QUIZZES

ARE YOU A SECRET KEEPER OR BiG BLABBERMOUTH?

CHECK OUT THESE SITCHES TO SEE IF YOU HAVE LOOSE LIPS!

1. There's some gossip spreading around school. **You**

A. forget about it. Gossip stinks.

B. try to find out more deets. Is it true or not?

C. only let your close friends know. They won't tell anyone, right?

2. You find out you won a huge award at school. **You**

A. let your parents know a couple days after you find out. No biggie.

B. tell your close friends but ask them not to make a big deal of it.

C. text and tell absolutely everyone. Even the janitor knows.

3. Your BFF confides in you about her latest crush. **You**

A. keep it to yourself. That's what friends do.

B. tell another good friend and ask her to promise not to tell a soul.

C. let her crush know. He should know she likes him!

4. A friend says your BFF can't keep a secret. **You**

A. don't repeat it. It will hurt your BFF's feelings.

B. keep it to yourself but suggest your friend talk to your BFF face-to-face if she has a problem with her.

C. tell your BFF immediately. She needs to know what people think of her.

5. There's a surprise party planned for a relative. **You**

A. are sworn to secrecy. You take surprises super seriously.

B. struggle keeping it to yourself. You drop major hints in front of your family member.

C. are so excited you spill the beans.

Turn page for answers

IF YOU ANSWERED MOSTLY ...

 **A's** then you rock, super secret keeper! Your friends, family, and everyone else will respect you for keeping your lips sealed.

 **B's** you might be trying not to be a big gossip, but you still need some work. Be mature and keep any rumors you hear to yourself.

 **C's** it sounds like you have a mouth that's a bit blabby. Yikes! If you want to make new friends and keep the old, you need to get your loose lips under control.

SUPE EMBARRASSING MOMENTS
YOU WISH YOU COULD HAVE KEPT SECRET

ASK YOURSELF. ASK YOUR FRIENDS.

Have you ever . . .

1. snorted when you laughed? ○ Yes ○ No

2. walked out of a restroom with toilet paper stuck to your shoe? ○ Yes ○ No

3. texted a message to someone who shouldn't have seen it? ○ Ugh, yes! ○ No

4. sent an embarrassing message thanks to auto correct? ○ Ahh! Yes! ○ No

5. fallen down in public? ○ Yes ○ No

6. had food stuck in your teeth and no one told you? ○ Yes ○ No

7. spit food out by accident when you were talking? ○ Yes ○ No

8. walked around with your zipper down? ○ Yes ○ No

9. accidentally walked into the boy's bathroom? ○ Yes ○ No

10. run up behind someone, called her name, and discovered she was
    the wrong person? ○ Yes ○ No

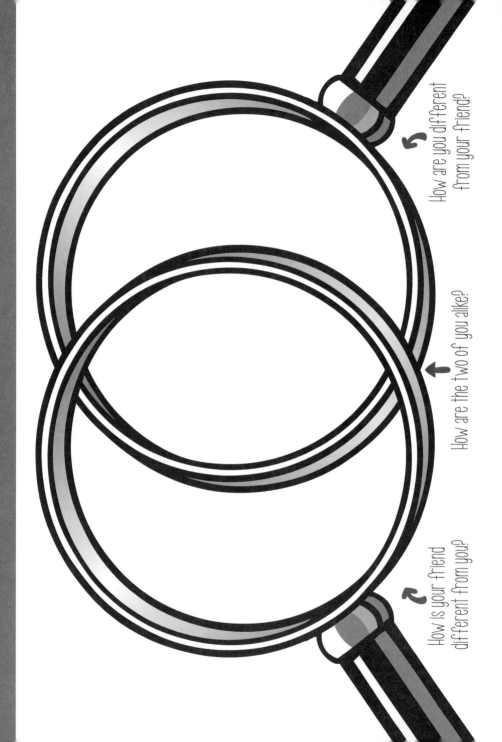

How are you different from your friend?

How are the two of you alike?

How is your friend different from you?

MYSTERIES

SEE HOW FAST YOU CAN SOLVE THESE MYSTERIES

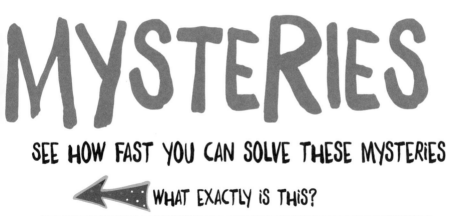 WHAT EXACTLY IS THIS?

WHAT DO YOUR TEACHERS DO WHEN THEY'RE NOT IN SCHOOL?

WHY IS YOUR ELBOW CALLED THE FUNNY BONE?

WHAT MAKES PINK LEMONADE PINK?

SECRET AGENT ROLE

DISCOVER A ROLE FOR YOURSELF ON A SECRET AGENT TEAM.
FINISH SOME THOUGHTS. ANSWER SOME QUESTIONS.
REVEAL THE UNDERCOVER YOU.

1. You have some free time, so you decide to

A. go shopping. You can't wait to see the hottest styles.

B. work out, play a sport, or work on some cool dance move.

C. chill out with a book. There's a bestseller you've been dying to read.

2. Which would you more likely be caught wearing?

A. Latest trendy clothes with super cute shoes

B. T-shirt and jeans

C. Cardi with a pretty blouse

3. Finish this sentence – I would love to

A. win a total makeover and spa day.

B. learn to walk across a tightrope.

C. assist a famous Loch Ness monster tracker.

4. Which free class or lesson would you sign up for?

A. Hair-braiding and up-dos

B. Karate

C. Conversational French

5. It's the night before a test. You

A. study before checking out your latest fashion magazine.

B. squeeze in some studying before working out.

C. study. Then study some more, just in case.

Turn page for answers

IF YOU ANSWERED MOSTLY ...

 **A's** get your cutest outfit, makeup, and curling iron out. You're the beautiful distraction that will lure villains to a trap. Whoa, what just hit them?!

 **B's** you might want to enroll in some kickboxing and jujitsu classes. Your super agent team is counting on your ninja-like moves. Look out bad guys!

 **C's** you better iron your lab coat. You'll be doing suspicious character background checks one day and studying unknown substances under a microscope the next. Get your geek on girl!

NOW YOU NEED A
SECRET AGENT iDENTiTY

1. CHOOSE A TITLE. ○ MISS ○ MS. ○ DR.

2. PICK ONE WORD.

SELENA	PETUNIA	PENNY
CHAMOMILE	SKYLAR	FELICITY
APPLE	WILLOW	DAFFODIL

3. PICK ANOTHER WORD (OR WORDS).

FOX	FITZSIMMONS	PINK
BLACK	STELLAR	SNOW LEOPARD
SPIDER LILY	DIAMONDBACK	WREN

4. WHAT'S YOUR FAVORITE LETTER? ☐

5. HOW ABOUT YOUR FAVORITE NUMBER? ☐

STRING IT ALL TOGETHER FOR YOUR NEW SECRET AGENT IDENTITY!

⬭ ⬭ ⬭

I. TITLE 2. WORD 3. WORD

A.K.A. AGENT ⬭ ⬭

4. LETTER 5. NUMBER

IF YOUR FRIENDS WERE

SECRET AGENTS

WHAT WOULD BE THEIR COOL NAMES?

COMBINE SOME OF THESE WORDS, LETTERS, AND NUMBERS TO MAKE AMAZING SECRET AGENT NAMES. OR, COME UP WITH YOUR OWN.

AGENT	KITTY	DIAMONDS	STAR
LADY	URSULA	SHADOW	W
CALLISTA	16	Z	BLAIR
MS.	POWERS	008	M
MADEMOISELLE	MIDNIGHT	VIPER	STINGRAY

FRIENDS' NAMES   *new* SECRET AGENT NAMES

FRiENDS' SECRETS
& NOT-SO-SECRETS

DO YOU KNOW WHAT YOUR FRiENDS LOVE, ABSOLUTELY DON'T LOVE, OR MAYBE SECRETLY LOVE? PUT YOURSELF TO THE TEST.

1. USiNG YOUR iNViSiBLE iNK PEN, TRY TO ANSWER THESE QUESTIONS JUST THE WAY YOUR FRiENDS WOULD.

2. THEN LET YOUR FRiENDS ANSWER THE QUESTIONS FOR THEMSELVES WiTH REGULAR PENS.

3. SHiNE YOUR PEN LiGHT ON YOUR iNViSiBLE ANSWERS FOR THE BiG REVEAL!

Make it invisible!

WHAT IS _____'s FAVE...
FRIEND'S NAME

HOW YOU THINK YOUR
FRIEND WOULD ANSWER ⟶ ⟵ FRIEND'S ACTUAL ANSWER

PART OF A CUPCAKE? _____   _____

SONG RIGHT NOW? _____   _____

THING ABOUT SCHOOL? _____   _____

WORD OR SAYING? _____   _____

COLOR? _____   _____

THING TO DO WITH FRIENDS? _____   _____

MOVIE? _____   _____

OUTFIT IN HER CLOSET? _____   _____

FOOD TO SNACK ON? _____   _____

PLACE TO HANG OUT? _____   _____

Turn page for more

WHICH WOULD _____ CHOOSE?

HOW YOU THINK YOUR
FRIEND WOULD ANSWER ↘   ↙ FRIEND'S
                                  ACTUAL ANSWER

CREAMY OR CRUNCHY? _____   _____

MALL OR OUTLET? _____   _____

FRO-YO OR ICE CREAM? _____   _____

SMALL   DEEP
TALK OR CONVERSATION? _____   _____

SUNRISE OR SUNSET? _____   _____

POLKA DOTS OR STRIPES? _____   _____

BEACH OR MOUNTAINS? _____   _____

CHIPS OR FRIES? _____   _____

SPEND OR SAVE? _____   _____

FEARLESS OR CAUTIOUS? _____   _____

HOW WOULD _____ ANSWER?

FRIEND'S NAME

HOW YOU THINK YOUR
FRIEND WOULD ANSWER

FRIEND'S
ACTUAL ANSWER

FAVORITE ACTRESS? _____ _____

BROWNIES OR COOKIES? _____ _____

BEST SMOOTHIE FLAVOR? _____ _____

MORNING   NIGHT
GLORY OR OWL? _____ _____

WHAT ARE YOU
AN EXPERT AT? _____ _____

WHAT DO YOU STINK AT? _____ _____

CAMPING OR POSH SUITE? _____ _____

WORRY   WORRY
WART OR FREE? _____ _____

FAVORITE BAND? _____ _____

TV OR BOOK? _____ _____

SiLLY SECR

ASK YOURSELF. ASK YOUR FRIENDS.

1. SOMETHING RIDICULOUS YOU'RE TOTES FRIGHTENED OF?

2. LAST DUMB THING YOU DID?

3. SOMEONE YOU DIDN'T LIKE AT FIRST BUT NOW YOU DO?

4. MOST EMBARRASSING THING THAT'S EVER HAPPENED TO YOU?

5. SOMETHING CRAZY YOU BELIEVED WHEN YOU WERE LITTLE?

6. SOMETHING CRAZY YOU BELIEVE IN NOW?

7. SOMETHING STINKY YOU LOVE TO EAT?

8. HOW DO YOU REALLY FEEL ABOUT YOUR FIRST NAME?

9. OUTFIT YOU CAN'T BELIEVE YOU EVER WORE?

ETS

10. DO YOU
HAVE A CRUSH?
○ NO ○ YES

MISSION IMPOSSIBLE
OR
MISSION POSSIBLE?

1. YOU'RE LOCKED OUT OF YOUR HOUSE SO YOU

A. walk to your friend's house and wait until your parents get home.

B. check all the doors and windows to make sure there's not another way in.

C. look in the the shed and find whatever you need to break in (minus the breaking part).

2. YOU AND YOUR FRIENDS DEVOUR A CAKE LEFT ON THE KITCHEN COUNTER. YOUR BRO TELLS YOU LATER IT WAS FOR YOUR MOM'S OFFICE PARTY THAT NIGHT. YOU

A. call her and tell her how sorry you are.

B. look up a recipe and bake another cake.

C. tell your sob story to your friend's mom who feels so badly for you that she bakes another cake for you.

3. YOUR FAMiLY iS CAUGHT iN TRAFFiC, AND THE SCHOOL DANCE STARTS iN 15 MiNUTES. YOU'RE iN A T-SHiRT AND SHORTS. YOU

A. complain for the rest of the trip home and decide to stay home.

B. swing by your house, grab a dress, and slip it on in the car as your mom drives you to school. You tell everyone that messy hair, no makeup, and arriving epically late to a dance is all the rage in Europe.

C. call your friends and ask them to meet you at school with an extra dress, curling iron, and makeup. The three of you can get you ready in no time!

4. YOU SPOT YOUR CRUSH AT THE MOVIE THEATER THE DAY AFTER YOU EMBARRASSED YOURSELF iN FRONT OF HiM AT SCHOOL. YOU DO NOT WANT HiM TO SEE YOU! YOU

A. immediately bolt. You hope he doesn't see you!.

B. put an empty popcorn box over your head and exit right before the closing credits start.

C. wait until the end and then ask your friend to get up and pretend to stumble, causing a major diversion, as you sneak out in the other direction.

5. YOU'VE BEEN OFFERED A CHOiCE OF THREE AWESOME SUMMER VACATiONS. PiCK ONE.

A. Hanging out with friends at a beach condo.

B. Traveling to Europe as a foreign exchange student.

C. Searching for lost treasure with a research team on a remote island in the Pacific.

Turn page for answers

IF YOU ANSWERED MOSTLY ...

 **A**s you're definitely Mission Impossible. You might just want to stick to watching spy movies. Maybe you'll learn a thing or two.

 **B**s you're Mission Maybe Possible. Start off in the secret agent office first before diving in.

 **C**s you're Mission Possible and ready for your first assignment. Congratulations Agent Awesome-sauce! Now go rock a super cool pair of shades.

HOW AWESOME CAN YOUR

SPY?

TRY TO FIND A
BOWTIE, MONACLE, CROWN, HARLEQUIN MASK, BIRTHDAY HAT,
MICROPHONE, ICE CREAM CONE, SNORKEL, & SWIMMNG MASK.

GIVE THESE CHARACTERS

HIDE THEIR IDENTITIES WITH SUNGLASSES, MASKS, MUSTACHES, HATS, & MORE

UNDERCOVER DISGUISES

Make it invisible!

PAY AT

TEST YOUR SLEUTHY OBSERVATION SKILLS. TRY TO REMEMBER WHAT KIDS WORE IN CLASS YESTERDAY.

NAME	WHAT HE/SHE WORE

ENTION!

OK, NOW TRY AGAIN ANOTHER DAY. REALLY LOOK AT WHAT EVERYONE'S WEARING. THEN WRITE IT DOWN AFTER CLASS.

NAME	WHAT HE/SHE WORE

Did you get any better?

HOLD THIS MESSAGE UP
TO A MIRROR TO DECODE.

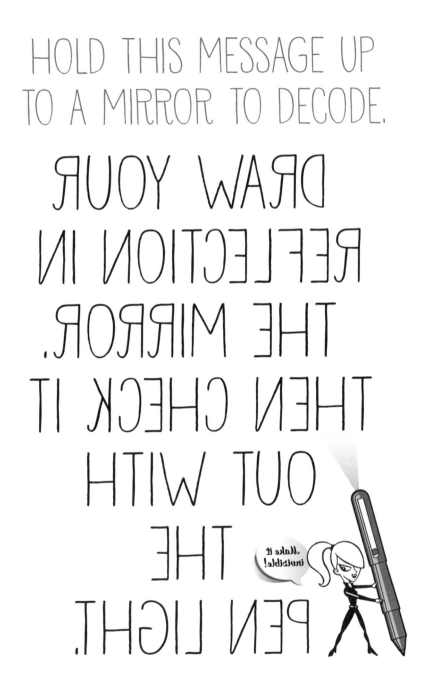

STUDY YOUR
FRIENDS & FAMILY

WATCH YOUR FAMILY,
FRIENDS, CRUSH, NEIGHBOR,
& DOG FOR A WHILE.

WHAT NERVOUS HABITS DO THEY HAVE?
WHAT WORDS DO THEY LOVE TO USE?
WHAT DO THEY WEAR A LOT?
WHAT DO THEY SMELL LIKE?

Make it invisible!

NAME   DESCRIPTION

COME UP WITH SECRET CODE WORDS OR SAYINGS TO USE IN PUBLIC WITH FRIENDS.

Make it invisible!

CODE WORD/SAYING

WHAT IT MEANS

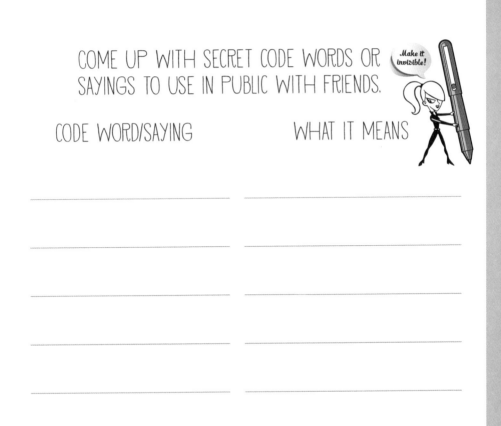

Zebra wing butterfly.

Yay, my crush just walked in.

HIDE STUFF FROM YOUR NOSY BROS, SISTERS, & FRIENDS, STASH YOUR THINGS. THEN DRAW A MAP OF WHERE EVERYTHING IS HIDDEN.

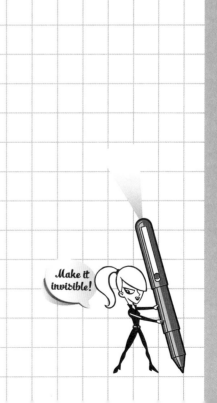

Make it invisible!

CREATE AN AMAZING SUNDAE. WITH A SECRET INGREDIENT.

KEEP THE RECIPE STASHED AWAY HERE.

Make it
invisible!

→ WRITE DOWN EVERYTHING YOU REMEMBER ABOUT THE PICTURE.

_____

_____

_____

_____

TRY AGAIN. LOOK AT THE PIC LIKE AN INVESTIGATOR. WRITE DOWN MORE DEETS.

_____

_____

_____

_____

YOU'RE NOW A PRIVATE  IN THE MAKING. STUDY THIS SCENE FOR 1 MINUTE. THEN TURN THE PAGE.

➤ TAKE NOTES ON EVERYTHING YOU REMEMBER ABOUT THE SCENE.

_____

_____

_____

_____

NOW TURN THIS PAGE UPSIDE DOWN AND AND ANSWER SOME QUESTIONS ABOUT THE SCENE.

IS THE SUN OR MOON PART OF THE SCENE?

HOW MANY CAMERAS?

WHAT KIND OF FLOWER APPEARS?

HOW MANY PAIRS OF GLASSES, INCLUDING SUNGLASSES?

NAME OF ONE STREET SIGN?

IF SOMEONE WERE SPYING

ON YOU TODAY WHAT WOULD YOU BE CAUGHT DOING?

@ 6:30 A.M. ───

───

@ 9:15 A.M. ───

───

@ 11:10 A.M. ──

───

@ 1:27 P.M. ───

───

@ 3:59 P.M. ───

───

@ 7:32 P.M. ───

───

@ 10:41 P.M. ──

───

What's the prob?

_____

_____

_____

_____

_____

_____

How will you solve it?

_____

_____

_____

_____

_____

_____

_____

What are some things you own that give clues to your true personality?

Stuff	What it says about you

My smelly sneakers say I love sports.

My red dress says I'm super girly.

IF YOU COULD GO UNDERCOVER AS A NEW KID AT SCHOOL WHAT WOULD YOU DO?

Try out for cheerleading again.

Find out what my friends really think about me.

Make friends with a totally new group of kids.

Share all the deets starting from now back to this morning. What'd you do? Who'd you see? Who'd you talk to?

_____

_____

_____

_____

_____

_____

_____

_____

_____

_____

_____

_____

_____

IF YOU LED A DOUBLE LIFE

DOUBLE LIFE

WHAT WOULD

YOUR

OTHER

LIFE BE

LIKE?

What would be your name?

Where would you live?

What would you do?

WHAT IS YOUR MISSION FOR TODAY?

Figure out how to get out of doing chores. Ace my math test. Get Josh to notice me.

Stuff you love but you'll never admit

Stuff you hate but you'll never tell

IF YOU COULD BE
INVISIBLE
WHAT WOULD YOU DO TODAY?

SEND SECRET MESSAGES

SEND SUPER SECRET NOTES!

Make it invisible!

Write notes to your friends. Then let your friends borrow your pen so they can read your messages.

Besties Secret PassNote

Besties Secret PassNote

Besties Secret PassNote

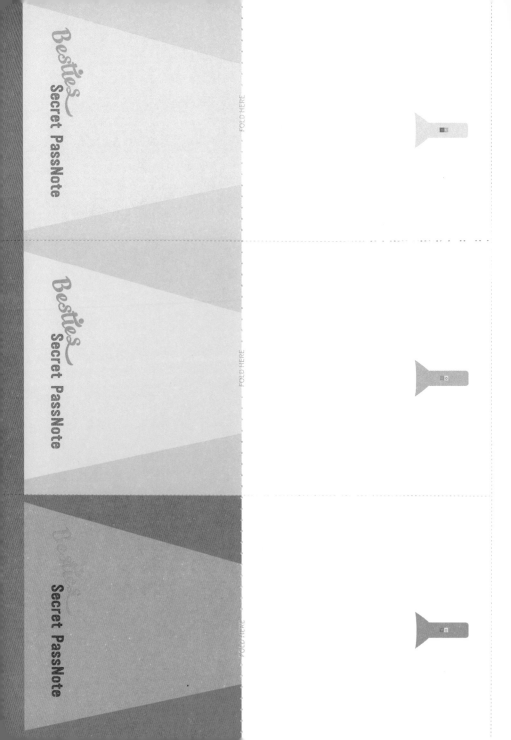

Besties Secret PassNote

Besties Secret PassNote

Besties Secret PassNote

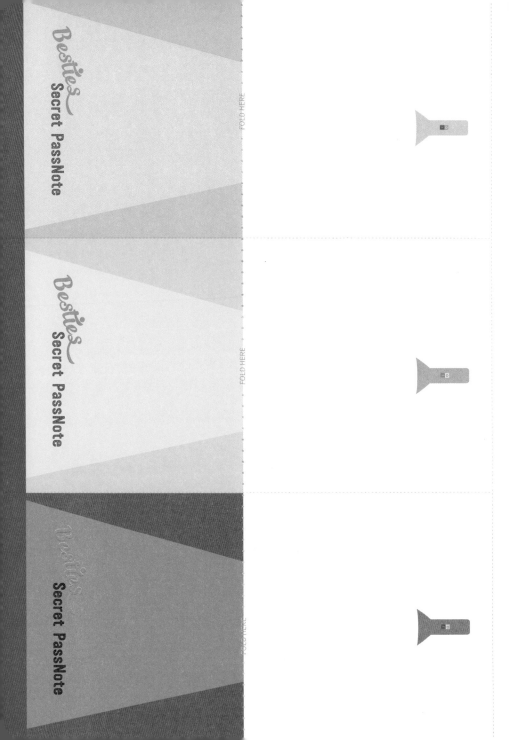

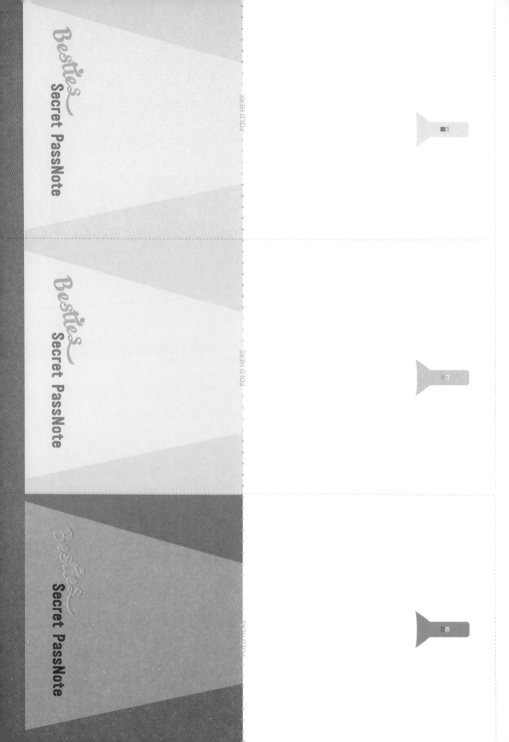

Besties Secret PassNote

Besties Secret PassNote

Besties Secret PassNote

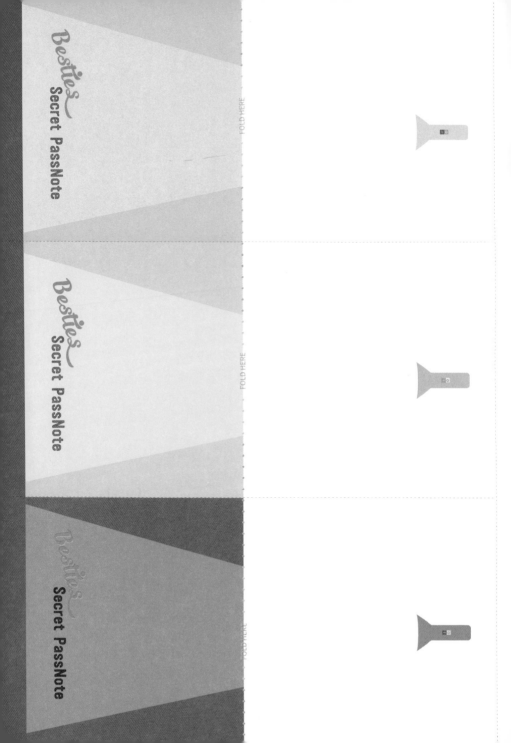

You Need A SECRET Friend CODE

Turn the page to start a cool code

Replace the letters of the alphabet with numbers, symbols, doodles, or other letters.

Write or draw your code below.

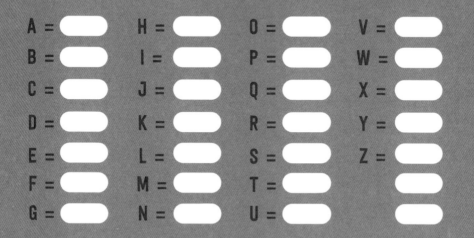

A = ◻
B = ◻
C = ◻
D = ◻
E = ◻
F = ◻
G = ◻

H = ◻
I = ◻
J = ◻
K = ◻
L = ◻
M = ◻
N = ◻

O = ◻
P = ◻
Q = ◻
R = ◻
S = ◻
T = ◻
U = ◻

V = ◻
W = ◻
X = ◻
Y = ◻
Z = ◻
◻
◻

Secret **Friend** Code

Keep in a safe **place. Expect a note written** in **code** soon!

A = _____   H = _____   O = _____   V = _____
B = _____   I = _____   P = _____   W = _____
C = _____   J = _____   Q = _____   X = _____
D = _____   K = _____   R = _____   Y = _____
E = _____   L = _____   S = _____   Z = _____
F = _____   M = _____   T = _____
G = _____   N = _____   U = _____

Secret **Friend** Code

Keep in a safe **place. Expect a note written** in **code** soon!

A = _____   H = _____   O = _____   V = _____
B = _____   I = _____   P = _____   W = _____
C = _____   J = _____   Q = _____   X = _____
D = _____   K = _____   R = _____   Y = _____
E = _____   L = _____   S = _____   Z = _____
F = _____   M = _____   T = _____
G = _____   N = _____   U = _____

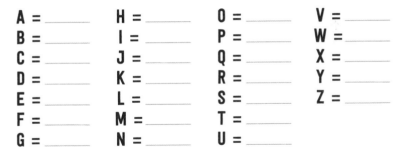

Secret **Friend** Code

Keep in a safe **place. Expect a note written** in **code** soon!

A = _____   H = _____   O = _____   V = _____
B = _____   I = _____   P = _____   W = _____
C = _____   J = _____   Q = _____   X = _____
D = _____   K = _____   R = _____   Y = _____
E = _____   L = _____   S = _____   Z = _____
F = _____   M = _____   T = _____
G = _____   N = _____   U = _____

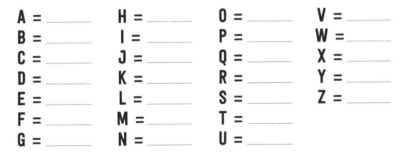

ULTRA TOP SECRET

YOUR SECRETS SAFE WITH ME

FOR YOUR EYES ONLY

FOLD HERE

FOLD HERE

FOLD HERE

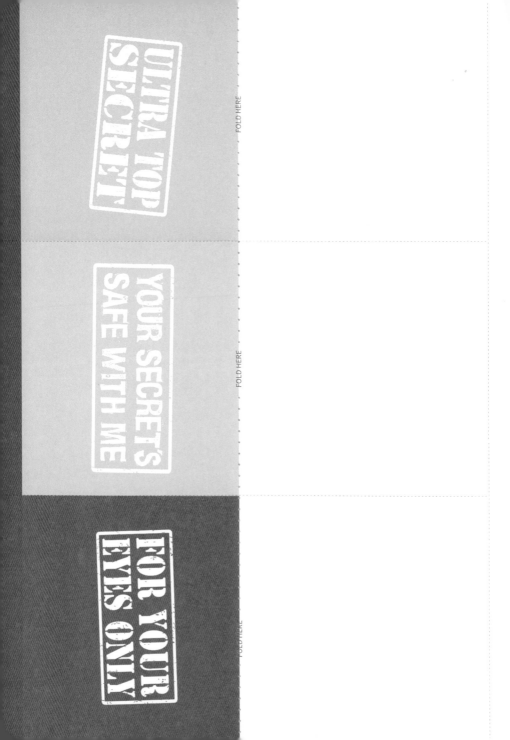

IF YOU LOVE THIS BOOK, CHECK OUT THESE COKE OR PEPSI? BOOKS!